Marx, Lenin, and Jesus:
Communism or the Bible?

by David E. Pratte

Available in print at
www.gospelway.com/sales

Marx, Lenin, and Jesus:
Communism or the Bible?

ISBN: 9798667323945
Imprint: Independently published

Note carefully: No teaching in any of our materials is intended or should ever be construed to justify or to in any way incite or encourage personal vengeance or physical violence against any person.

**"He who glories, let him glory in the Lord"
– 1 Corinthians 1:31**

Romans 1:20 – "For since the creation of the world His invisible attributes are clearly seen, being understood by the things that are made, even His eternal power and Godhead, so that they are without excuse." (NKJV)

Acknowledgements
Front page photo and all photos are public domain via Pixabay, Pixnio, and Wikimedia

Unless otherwise indicated, Scripture quotations are generally from the New King James Version (NKJV), copyright 1982, 1988 by Thomas Nelson, Inc. used by permission. All rights reserved.

Scripture quotations marked (NASB) are from *Holy Bible, New American Standard* La Habra, CA: The Lockman Foundation, 1995.

Scripture quotations marked (ESV) are from *The Holy Bible, English Standard Version*, copyright ©2001 by Crossway Bibles, a publishing ministry of Good News Publishers. Used by permission. All rights reserved.

Scripture quotations marked (NRSV) are from the New Revised Standard Version of the Bible, copyright 1989 by the Division of Christian Education, National Council of the Churches of Christ in the United States of America.

Scripture quotations marked (NIV) are from the New International Version of the Holy Bible, copyright 1978 by Zondervan Bible publishers, Grand Rapids, Michigan.

Scripture quotations marked (HCSB) are from the Holman Christian Standard Bible, copyright 2008 by Holman Bible publishers, Nashville, Tennessee.

Scripture quotations marked (MLV) are from Modern Literal Version of The New Testament, Copyright 1999 by G. Allen Walker.

Other Books by the Author

Topical Bible Studies

Why Believe in God, Jesus, and the Bible? (evidences)
True Words of God: Bible Inspiration and Preservation
"It Is Written": The Authority of the Bible
Salvation through Jesus Christ: Basics of Forgiveness
Grace, Faith, and Obedience: The Gospel or Calvinism?
Growing a Godly Marriage & Raising Godly Children
The God of the Bible (study of the Father, Son, and Holy Spirit)
"In the Beginning God Created..." (creation vs. evolution)
Kingdom of Christ: Future Millennium or Present Spiritual Reign?
Do Not Sin Against the Child: Abortion, Unborn Life, & the Bible
Marx, Lenin, and Jesus: Communism or the Bible?

Commentaries on Bible Books

Genesis	*Proverbs*	*Ephesians*
Joshua and Ruth	*Ecclesiastes*	*Philippians &*
Judges	*Daniel*	*Colossians*
1 Samuel	*Gospel of Matthew*	*1 & 2 Thessalonians*
2 Samuel	*Gospel of Mark*	*Hebrews*
1 Kings	*Gospel of John*	*James and Jude*
2 Kings	*Acts*	*1 and 2 Peter*
Ezra, Nehemiah, Esther	*Romans*	*1,2,3 John*
Job	*Galatians*	

Bible Question Class Books

Genesis	*Ecclesiastes*	*2 Corinthians and*
Joshua and Ruth	*Isaiah*	*Galatians*
Judges	*Daniel*	*Ephesians and*
1 Samuel	*Hosea, Joel, Amos,*	*Philippians*
2 Samuel	*Obadiah*	*Colossians, 1&2*
1 Kings	*Gospel of Matthew*	*Thessalonians*
2 Kings	*Gospel of Mark*	*1 & 2 Timothy,*
Ezra, Nehemiah,	*Gospel of Luke*	*Titus, Philemon*
Esther	*Gospel of John*	*Hebrews*
Job	*Acts*	*James – Jude*
Proverbs	*Romans*	*Revelation*
	1 Corinthians	

Workbooks with Study Notes

Jesus Is Lord: Workbook on the Fundamentals of the Gospel of Christ
Following Jesus: Workbook on Discipleship
God's Eternal Purpose in Christ: Workbook on the Theme of the Bible
Family Reading Booklist

**Visit our website at www.gospelway.com/sales to see a
current list of books in print.**

Other Resources from the Author

**Printed books, booklets, and tracts available at
www.gospelway.com/sales
Free Bible study articles online at
www.gospelway.com
Free Bible courses online at www.biblestudylessons.com
Free class books at
www.biblestudylessons.com/classbooks
Free commentaries on Bible books at
www.biblestudylessons.com/commentary
Contact the author at
www.gospelway.com/comments**

Abbreviations Used in These Notes

ASV – American Standard Version
b/c/v – book, chapter, and verse
ESV – English Standard Version
f – the following verse
ff – the following verses
HCSB – Holman Christian Standard Bible
KJV – King James Version
MLV – Modern Literal Version
NASB – New American Standard Bible
NEB – New English Bible
NIV – New International Version
NKJV – New King James Version
NRSV – New Revised Standard Version
RSV – Revised Standard Version

Note: Unless otherwise indicated, Bible quotations are from the New King James Version. Often - especially when I do not use quotations marks – I am not quoting any translation but simply paraphrasing the passage in my own words.

Table of Contents

(Due to printer reformatting, the above numbers may be off a page or two.)

The Doctrines of Marxism-Leninism

Introduction:

If we had lived before WWII, what should Christians have done about Nazism?

Suppose we were aware of the basic teachings of Nazism.

Should we have kept quiet because:

* It involved political and economic issues, but we are concerned only about religion?

* It controlled governments, but Christians should not criticize rulers?

* Speaking out might lead to persecution?

* It was mainly a problem elsewhere, not here (we didn't know many Nazis)?

Or, should we have spoken out to express opposition because:

* It was based on fundamental religious errors (evolution, racism, atheism)?

* It rejected Christianity and denied Jesus?

* It sought world domination by war and military conquest (subjugating millions by war)?

* It used violence and force to eliminate unwanted citizens (millions in the holocaust)?

2 Timothy 4:2-4; Ephesians 5:11; Revelation 3:19 – God's word instructs us to oppose the forces of evil. Surely we ought to have

reproved a belief based on religious error that forcibly subjugated millions of people and murdered millions more.

What should we do today about the growing menace of Islam?

Should we keep quiet because:

* It involves political and economic issues, but we are concerned only about religion?

* It controls governments, but Christians should not criticize rulers?

* Speaking out might lead to persecution?

* It is mainly a problem elsewhere (we don't know many Muslims)?

Or, should we speak out to express opposition because:

* It is based on fundamental religious errors (Muhammed, Quran)?

* It rejects Christianity and denies Jesus as the Son of God and Savior?

* It seeks world domination by war and military conquest (controlling millions worldwide)?

* It uses violence and force to make converts?

2 Timothy 4:2-4; Ephesians 5:11; Revelation 3:19 – Surely we all agree that, when God instructs us to oppose the forces of evil, we ought to reprove this system based on religious error that has forcibly subjugated millions of people.

Now what we should do about the problem of Marxism and Communism?

Should we keep quiet because:

* It involves political and economic issues, but we are concerned only about religion?

* It controls governments, but Christians should not criticize rulers?

* Speaking out might lead to persecution?

* We think it is mainly a problem elsewhere, (we don't know many Communists)?

Or, should we speak out to express opposition because:

* It is based on fundamental religious errors (atheism, evolution, immorality)?

* It rejects Christianity and Jesus?

* It seeks world domination by war and military conquest? (Communism controls over a billion people, nearly all of whom were subjugated through violent revolution. Open Communists admit they are enemies of the USA.)

* It uses violence and murder to eliminate unwanted citizens? (In every Communist nation, millions of people like you and me have been murdered by Communist leaders.)

Yet little is said by Christians about Communism. In fact, many members know little about it, yet it is at least as dangerous as Nazism and Islam.

2 Timothy 4:2-4; Ephesians 5:11; Revelation 3:19 – Again, God instructs us to oppose the forces of evil. Should we not speak against this system, based on religious error, that has forcibly subjugated millions of people and murdered millions more, like we should Nazism and Islam?

Is Communism a problem today?

Many people think Communism is no longer an issue because Russia renounced it. But the World Atlas (7/2020) listed the following countries as openly controlled by Marxist regimes (www.worldatlas.com/articles/list-of-communist-countries-today.html):

China – population 1.4 billion
Vietnam – 96 million
North Korea – 26 million
Cuba – 11 million (90 miles from our shore)
Laos – 7 million
(Population statistics from Wikipedia as of July, 2019)

But this is just the tip of the iceberg. Many other nations struggle with Communist subversion and internal turmoil. As we proceed we will observe examples of Communist influence in the world today.

The purpose of this study is to inform people about the real views of Communism, and how it differs from the gospel of Jesus.

Marxism-Leninism is not just about politics and economics. It is a total philosophy that affects every area of life, including many areas fundamental to Bible teaching. Marxism is a conspiracy that works by deceit, concealing its real goals until a nation is ready for a violent revolution. Meanwhile, many people have unknowingly been influenced by Marxist ideas.

What should a Christian do about this philosophy that forcibly dominates 1½ billion people and deceitfully influences the thinking of millions more? Should we not teach against it while we have the opportunity to do so openly? To begin with, we must learn to understand it.

(Note: See the bibliography at the end of this study for the sources we cite. Source notes in the text consist of a two- or three-digit code followed by a page number.)

Karl Marx.

I. Marxism and the Existence of God

Quotations Regarding Marxism

The founders of Marxism

Karl Marx was the primary promoter of the theories underlying modern Communism. He was an atheist even before he developed his Communistic theories. As the motto for his doctoral dissertation he chose a quote from Prometheus: "In simple truth, I harbour hate 'gainst all the Gods" (SC-25). His dissertation stated that we should "recognize as the highest divinity, the human self-consciousness itself!" He once planned to publish a Journal of Atheism but failed for lack of finances (NC-12f).

He said: "Communism begins where atheism begins." And "I wish to avenge myself against the One who rules above." (www.azquotes.com)

Friedrich Engels was probably Marx's greatest personal supporter. He and Marx collaborated in writing the *Communist Manifesto*. Engels was also an atheist. He stated that, as a result of the discovery of laws of Communism, "the last vestige of a Creator external to the world is obliterated" (NC-37).

Vladimir Lenin founded the Communist Party, led the Russian Communist revolution, and became the first premier of the Russian Communist regime. He was also an atheist. He said: "Atheism is a natural and inseparable part of Marxism, of the theory and practice of scientific socialism. Our program necessarily includes the propaganda of atheism." – Vladimir Lenin (www.azquotes.com)

And again: "Every religious idea, every idea of god, even every flirtation with the idea of God, is unutterable vileness" (REL-42).

Other Communist statements

Nikita Khrushchev, Russian premier from 1958 to 1964, stated:

> "We, Communists ... are atheists ... Public education, the dissemination of scientific knowledge, and the study of the laws of nature, leave no place for belief in God ... We consider that belief in God contradicts our Communist outlook" (BC-13).

He also said: "We remain the atheists that we have always been; we are doing all we can to liberate those people who are still under the spell of this religious opiate" (BC-73).

The *Russian Encyclopedia* (1950) lists: "God – a mythical invented being ... [Communism] is incompatible with belief in God; it arose and developed in an acute and constant struggle with religion" (BC-12).

The "Ten Commandments of Communism," published for the Young Communist League, says: "If you are not a convinced atheist, you cannot be a good Communist ... Atheism is indissolubly bound to Communism." (CFF-37).

Whittaker Chambers, a former Communist spy, said: "The problem of Communism is not an economic problem. The problem of Communism is the problem of atheism" (CFF-36).

Note clearly: ***Marxism is not primarily about economics or politics. Its fundamental beliefs relate to religion.*** The problem is more than just that some Communists are atheists. The problem is that atheism is fundamental to Communist belief.

As you consider our own society, how effective have Marxists and other unbelievers been in undermining faith in God? Do you see evidence of increasing faith or loss of faith?

Not every unbeliever is a Communist, but who can deny that our society is moving in the direction that Marxists want it to go? And as people become weaker in faith, it becomes more likely that Marxists can succeed with their goals.

The Teaching of the Bible

The Bible not only affirms the existence of God, but it also gives objective evidence, sufficient to satisfy any honest student, that God does exist and that the God of the Bible is the true God.

The Bible affirms God's existence.

Genesis 1:1 – In the beginning God created the heaven and the earth. From the first verse and throughout its teaching the Bible claims that God does exist.

Hebrews 11:6 – Without faith it is impossible to please God. We must believe that He is and that He is a rewarder of those who diligently seek Him.

Psalms 14:1 – The fool has said in his heart, "There is no God." So a Christian, who believes the Bible, must conclude that Communism is foolish.

Obviously, a person cannot be an atheist and a believer at the same time. To be a Communist you must be (or must become) an atheist. To be a Christian you must be a believer. It follows that one cannot be both a true Communist and a true Christian.

The Bible provides evidence for God's existence.

Acts 14:17 – God did not leave Himself without witness. The Bible does not just claim that God exists. It also gives witness or evidence for the claim.

The Bible itself proves God's existence, for mere men cannot write such a book as the Bible, nor could mere men do the miracles that eyewitnesses record in the Bible. We will consider this evidence later. But notice here some evidence offered in nature for the existence of God.

Romans 1:18-22 – God has made known the evidence for His power and Godhead. That evidence may be seen in the things that are made, so there is no excuse for people who do not believe. Yet people refuse to glorify Him as God or be thankful to Him. By relying on their human wisdom, they become foolish. This surely describes Communism. The proof that God exists, and therefore Marxism is wrong, may be seen in the universe.

Psalms 19:1 – The heavens declare the glory of God and the firmament shows His handiwork. There is simply no reasonable explanation for the existence of the things we see in nature except that there is a Supreme Being, far wiser and more powerful than we are, who made them.

Because we are intelligent beings, we can recognize the fruits of intelligence. Anyone who examines computers, cameras, automobiles, houses, etc., can know that they must have been made by intelligent beings. But the same is true of the human brain, eye, reproductive system, and our whole bodies, as well as all other living beings.

Every effect must have an adequate cause: an adequate explanation. The only adequate explanation for the universe is God. Do Marxists have adequate proof that God does not exist? Do they have an adequate explanation for the existence of the universe without God? As we proceed we will see that their explanation is evolution, but that is not an adequate explanation for all we see around us.

Surely our country is being influenced by unbelief. Not every atheist is a Marxist, but Marxism is fundamentally atheistic. Marxism promotes atheism, and unbelief leads people to accept a major doctrine of Marxism. Surely the fact that Marxism is fundamentally atheistic is one reason for us to oppose it.

To learn more about the evidence for the existence of God and the Bible as His word, please study our free

articles on that subject on our Bible study web site at www.gospelway.com/instruct (see the section about God/Deity).

Charles Darwin

II. Marxism and the Origin of Man

Quotations Regarding Marxism

Quotations from Marxist leaders

In the preface to the **Communist Manifesto**, Engels said that the basic theory of Communism "is destined to do for history what Darwin's theory has done for biology" (CM-3,4). Obviously, he believed Darwin's view of evolution just as he believed Marx's theory of Communism.

A few months after Darwin published his *Origin of Species*, **Engels** wrote to Marx saying, "Darwin, whom I am just now reading, is splendid."

Later **Marx** wrote to Engels saying that Darwin's book: "...contains the basis in natural history for our view." Soon afterward Marx wrote: "Darwin's book is very important and serves me as a basis in natural science for the class struggle in history." In fact, Marx wanted to dedicate his book *Das Kapital* to Darwin. (*Impact*, 10/87)

Lenin said: "Darwin put an end to the belief that animal and vegetable species ... were created by God..." (*Impact*, 10/87).

Fundamentals of Marxism-Leninism states: "Nature ... is in constant process of development. The laws of that development have not been ordained by God ... They are intrinsic in nature itself..." (FML-16).

Josef **Stalin** was secretary-general of the Communist Party and Russian premier until 1953. A Communist named Yaroslavsky, in his biography of Stalin, says: "At a very early age ... Comrade Stalin developed a critical mind and revolutionary sentiments. He began to read Darwin and became an atheist."

The biography records this boyhood conversation: "'You know, they are fooling us, there is no God ... I'll lend you a book to read; it will show you that ... all this talk about God is sheer nonsense,' Joseph said. 'What book is that?' I enquired. 'Darwin. You must read it,' Joseph impressed on me" (via *Impact* 10/87; compare HRQ-53).

Again, the point is not just that some Communist leaders believe in evolution. The concern is that they view evolution as the basis for atheism and Communism.

How successful have Marxists and other unbelievers been in promoting evolution in our society? Do our schools and colleges teach evolution or creation?

In November, 2012, Chicagosocialists.org (an openly Marxist site) recorded that "Chicago district of the International Socialist Organization" conducted the "2012 Midwestern Marxism Conference" at Northwestern University. An observer noted that the Conference was attended by a significant number of members of the Chicago teachers' union, who had recently conducted a strike against Chicago schools. A number of them spoke or conducted workshops at the conference. – http://thunderontheright.wordpress.com/2012/12/06/marxism-in-chicago-schools/#more-1392 (11/19/2012)

Many other observers have reported significant numbers of Marxist teachers in our universities and colleges. (See Phyllis Schlafly, 4/10/2009; David A. Noebel, 10/11/2012).

Not every believer in evolution is a Communist, but who can deny that our society is moving in the direction that Marxists want it to go? And as evolution becomes more accepted, it becomes more likely that Marxists can succeed with their goals.

The Teachings of the Bible

The Bible says God created all forms of life.

Genesis 1:1; Acts 17:24-28 – The Bible claims that life was created by God. One cannot accept both the Communist view and the Bible view: it must be one or the other.

Further, the Bible view harmonizes with the scientific truth that life comes from life. But evolution requires that dead, non-living matter must somehow have spontaneously produced life and intelligence. This is unscientific. Science has repeatedly disproved spontaneous generation. Yet Communism claims it is scientific and the Bible is not.

The Bible says living things reproduce after their own kind.

Genesis 1:11,21,24f; Galatians 6:7 – God made living things to reproduce after their own kind. Living things can adapt to their environment, but they cannot produce totally different kinds, such that all present kinds came from one or a few original kinds.

This also harmonizes with scientific evidence. Current observations show that living things reproduce after their kind. Further, if evolution were true, the fossil record should show numerous transitional links that are halfway between present kinds. But the links are missing.

The Bible says man is unique from the animals.

Genesis 1:26-28 – Man is in the image of God, unique and superior to the animals. The first human did not develop from animals but was created directly by God from the earth (2:7).

Simple observation confirms the differences between men and animals. No animals can read and write abstract symbols to communicate messages or perform mathematical calculations. No animals do scientific experiments, invent machines, use fire, or train animals. No animal creates new forms of beauty nor has an inherent sense of morals and conscience as man does.

These differences are easily explained if man was created in God's image, as the Bible says. But evolution cannot explain why men are so different from the animals from which we supposedly evolved.

Again, Communism cannot be harmonized with the gospel of Christ. But when schools teach evolution, they encourage young people to become atheists. This, in turn, inclines them to accept Communism, as in the case of Stalin. What are you doing to prevent this from happening to your children?

Surely the fact that Marxism is based on evolution is one reason for us to oppose it.

To learn more about the evidence for creation as opposed to evolution, please study our free articles on that subject on our Bible study web site at www.gospelway.com/instruct (see the section about God/Deity).

Lenin

III. Marxism and Materialism

Quotations Regarding Marxism

Fundamentals of Marxism-Leninism says: "The indestructible foundation of the whole edifice of Marxism-Leninism is its philosophy – dialectical and historical materialism" (FML -21). Furthermore:

> "Marxism-Leninism regards the world such as it actually is, without adding an invented hell or paradise. It proceeds from the fact that all nature, including man himself, consists of matter with its different properties ... There are no supernatural phenomena or forces, nor can be ... The great historic service rendered by materialist philosophy is that it helped man ... not to fear gods and other supernatural forces. It teaches us not to hope for happiness beyond the grave..." (FML-16,23,25).

Lenin said: "Our program is based entirely on scientific – to be more precise – upon a materialistic world conception" (REL-9). He added: "We must combat religion – this is the ABC of all materialism, and consequently Marxism" (REL-14).

Mao Zedong (Tse-tung) was chairman of the Chinese Communist Party from 1943 till his death. He said, "there is nothing in the world apart from matter in motion" (CFF-79).

Stalin said: "Marx's philosophical materialism holds ... that the world develops in accordance with the laws of movement of matter and stands in no need of a 'universal spirit'" (BC-22).

Khrushchev said: "Scientific and atheistic propaganda is an integral part of the Communist education ..., and has as its aim the dissemination of scientific, materialistic knowledge among the masses and the liberation of believers from the influence of religious prejudices" (BC-23).

So materialism is foundational to Marxism. It teaches that everything is material. There are no spirit beings, nothing about man that exists after death. So, there is no life after death, no heaven, no hell. It follows that no religion that believes in a spirit god can be true.

As you look at our society, how effective have Marxists and other unbelievers been in promoting materialism? Do you see people generally concerned about spiritual matters, or do you see an increasing emphasis on possessions, pleasure, and material things?

Obviously, not every materialistic person is a Communist, but who can deny that our society is moving in the direction that Marxists want it to go? And as people become more materialistic, it becomes more likely that Marxists can succeed with their goals.

The Teachings of the Bible

The Bible affirms that there are spirit beings and that in fact God is spirit.

God and spirit beings do exist.

John 4:24 – God is Spirit, and those who worship Him must worship in spirit and truth.

2 Corinthians 4:16-18 – Man consists of an outer man (body) and an inner man (spirit). The things we see (material things) are temporary. Yet there are eternal things we do not see.

Man exists after death as a spirit being and will be raised from the dead.

Matthew 22:23-32 – In Jesus' day the Sadducees were materialists who denied the spiritual aspect of man (Acts 23:6-10). Like modern materialists, they necessarily denied the resurrection. Jesus disagreed and showed that God spoke of Abraham, Isaac, and Jacob as living beings even though they had been dead for many years (verse 32). This could not be if a man is wholly "matter in motion."

Luke 16:19-31 – Jesus described dead men who were yet conscious and able to reason, remember, and communicate. This totally conflicts with materialism.

John 6:40,44,45; 5:28,29; Acts 24:15 – Jesus and His apostles often affirmed that all people will be raised from the dead. Man's spirit leaves his body at death (James 2:26) and then returns in the resurrection.

Materialists say death ends man's existence, and there is no spirit that could continue to exist or later return to the body. In affirming the resurrection, Jesus flatly contradicted fundamental Marxist doctrine.

The resurrection of Jesus proves our resurrection and disproves materialism.

1 Corinthians 15:1-26 – If, as Marxism says, there is no resurrection, then the gospel is false, the Christian's faith is worthless and the Christian's hope of reward after death is a false hope (verses 12-17; compare 1 Thessalonians 4:13-18). If Marxism is true, the gospel of Christ cannot be true. But if the gospel is true, then Communism cannot be true.

Verses 20-26 – How do we know we will be raised from the dead? Because Jesus was raised! His resurrection is the proof we will be raised.

Verses 1-8 – How do we know Jesus was raised? Because many eyewitnesses testified that they saw Him alive after His death.

John 20:24-31; 21:24 – The gospel records the testimony of many witnesses who saw Jesus alive after His resurrection. This testimony is as valid as historical testimony in any courtroom. (Compare Matthew 27 & 28; Mark 15 & 16; Luke 23 & 24; John 19, 20, & 21; Acts 1 & 9.)

This is why all materialists vehemently deny Jesus' resurrection. Yet the fact remains that no Marxist can prove that materialism is true. Which of them can state for certain that man has no existence after death?

The strongest proof that materialism is false is Jesus' resurrection. Someone has already come back from the dead! This is simple historical proof that Communists cannot invalidate.

Surely the fact that Marxism is fundamentally materialistic is one reason for us to oppose it.

Mao

IV. Marxism and Religion

Quotations regarding Marxism

Several previous quotations show that Communists do not believe in God or the Bible. They oppose religion because it keeps people from accepting Communism. Note the evidence:

Statements from Marxist leaders

Asked what his objective in life was, **Marx** replied: "To dethrone God and destroy capitalism" (NC-37).

He also said: "Religion is the opium of the masses." "The first requisite for the happiness of the people is the abolition of religion." "... Communism abolishes eternal truths, it abolishes all religion, and all morality ..." www.azquotes.com

According to Lenin: "Marx said 'Religion is the opium of the people' – and this postulate is the cornerstone of the whole philosophy of Marxism with regard to religion. Marxism always regarded all modern religions and churches, and every kind of religious organisation [sic] as instruments of that bourgeois reaction whose aim is to defend exploitation by stupefying the working-class" (REL-12).

Lenin also said: "Marxism is materialism. As such it is ... relentlessly opposed to religion ... This is beyond doubt ... We must combat religion – this is the A.B.C. of all materialism, and consequently of Marxism" (REL-14) "There can be nothing more abominable than religion." (www.azquotes.com)

Stalin said: "The Party cannot be neutral towards religion, and it does conduct anti-religious propaganda against all and every religious prejudice because it stands for science, while ... all religion is something opposite to science" (CFF-164; BC- 12).

And "By May, 1st, 1937, there should not be one single church left within the borders of Soviet Russia, and the idea of God will have been banished from the Soviet Union..." Joseph Stalin:: www.azquotes.com

The Sixth World Congress of the Communist International stated: "One of the most important tasks of the cultural revolution affecting the wide masses is the task of systematically and unswervingly combating religion – the opium of the people" (REL-6).

In countries where they are not in power, Marxists seek to infiltrate the institutions of society to undermine Biblical and religious ideas. This includes infiltrating government, schools, and churches themselves.

Communists especially try to influence young people. So they seek to eliminate the Bible and prayer from schools, while also encouraging schools to advocate evolution, feminism, homosexuality, abortion, and other anti-biblical views. How effective have they (and other liberal-thinking people) have been in the USA?

Note the following from *Phyllis Schlafly Report*, 11/2010:

The most widely used history textbook in U.S. public schools is *A People's History of the United States* by the late Howard Zinn. It has sold a million and a half copies since it was published in 1980. It is required reading in many high schools and colleges.

This history textbook by Howard Zinn is a very leftwing version of U.S. history, full of multicultural, feminist, and class-war propaganda. ...

In 2010, the FBI released 400 pages of files on Howard Zinn, and it turns out that he was an active member of the Communist Party. He ... attended Communist Party meetings in Brooklyn five nights a week. He was so important in the Communist Party that he taught a class to his comrades on "basic Marxism." ... Publicly, Howard Zinn lied and denied his Communist Party membership, which was the common practice of Communist Party members in those years.

...His textbook was specifically written to present a Marxist version of U.S. history based on the Communist strategy of the "class war."

Note regarding the reference to "multicultural propaganda": Multicultural teachings train students to believe all cultures are equal, including all religions.

As you view our society, do you see people who are increasingly concerned about religion, or are people increasingly indifferent toward religion? Do our schools and society in general show respect for religion or increasing disrespect?

Obviously, not every irreligious person is a Communist, but who can deny that our society is moving in the direction that Marxists want it to go? And as people become less religious, it becomes more likely that Marxists can succeed with their goals.

The Teaching of the Bible

The Bible affirms that it is a Divine revelation.

2 Timothy 3:16,17; 1 Corinthians 14:37 – The Bible is inspired by God. It instructs men in righteousness, provides to all good works, and contains the commandments of the Lord.
(Ephesians 3:3-5; 2 Peter 1:21; 1 Thessalonians 2:13)

The Bible gives evidence that it is a Divine revelation.

Luke 24:25-27,44; Acts 2:22-36; Deuteronomy 18:20-22 – The Bible gives good reasons to believe that it really is from God. Consider specifically the fact that Jesus and Bible writers were able to predict the future, and these predictions always came true. The Bible writers used this as evidence that God exists, that the Bible writers were from God, and that Jesus is the Son of God.

John 5:36; 20:26-31; Acts 14:3; 1 Corinthians 15:1-8 – The Bible includes eyewitness testimony that Jesus, His apostles, and other Bible writers did great miracles to demonstrate that God approved their message. These miracles were so powerful that even enemies of the gospel could not deny them (Acts 4:16; 8:5-13; John 11:47,48).

Much other evidence could be presented to confirm that the Bible is from God, that it is accurate historically, geographically, and scientifically, and that it does not contradict itself. **For further discussion of the evidence for God, Jesus, and the Bible, see our articles on that subject on our Bible Instruction web site at www.gospelway.com/instruct/.**

Since the gospel of Christ is true, Marxism and the gospel are incompatible.

1 Corinthians 1:18-25 – People who follow human wisdom consider the gospel to be foolish, but it is actually the power of God.

Ephesians 5:11 – We must not have fellowship with works of darkness, but rather reprove them.

You cannot be both a Communist and a Christian for at least two reasons: first because Communism says you cannot, and second because the gospel of Christ says you cannot. The two are mutually exclusive.

Surely the fact that Marxism is fundamentally anti-religious is one reason for us to oppose it.
(2 Corinthians 6:14-18)

Marxism - Leninism

Stalin

V. Marxism and Morality

Marxist Doctrine

Basic Marxist concepts

To understand Communist morality, we must consider the Marxist doctrine of the dialectic and class struggle. The fundamental belief is that people act primarily from economic motivations: to meet material needs and to accumulate material possessions. This is not a matter of choice. Basically, we are all machines whose conduct is determined entirely by economic conditions.

Classical Marxism says, at any given time in history, basically two economic classes exist: the ruling class and the oppressed class (the haves and the have-nots). The conflict between these classes inevitably builds until the oppressed class finally overthrows the ruling class. New classes then develop and the procedure is repeated over and over. The outcome of such conflicts always leads to improved conditions for mankind. This concept is called the dialectic or the class struggle.

Marxism affirms that, at the current stage of history, the two basic conflicting economic classes are the capitalists or the business owners (the bourgeoisie) and the workers employed by the owners (the proletariat). The conflict between these two classes must increase until the proletariat overthrows the capitalists. This outcome is inevitable, but the Communist Party exists to direct the efforts to hasten the victory of the proletariat over the capitalists.

How does this relate to morality? They deny the existence of God and of the Bible as a standard of right or wrong. So instead, any act that furthers the victory of the oppressed class over the ruling class is, by their definition, a moral act. Any act that hinders the victory of the oppressed class is an immoral act.

Since the Communist Party is responsible to direct the victory of the oppressed class, it follows that the teachings of Marx, Lenin, and the leaders of the Communist Party become the standard of morality.

Quotations regarding Marxist moral concepts

Lenin said:

"Is there such a thing as Communist morality? Of course there is ... In what sense do we repudiate ethics and morality? In the sense that they were preached by the bourgeoisie, who declared that ethics were God's commandments. We, of course, say that we do not believe in God ... And we subordinate our Communist morality to this [the class struggle]. We say: Morality is that which serves to destroy the old exploiting society and to unite all the toilers around the proletariat, which is creating a new Communist society. Communist morality is the morality which serves this struggle ... We do not believe in eternal morality ... At the basis of Communist morality lies the struggle for the consolidation and consummation of Communism" (SW9-474-479).

American Communist William Z. Foster said: "With him [the Communist] the end justifies the means. Whether his tactics be 'legal' or 'moral' or not, does not concern him, so long as they are effective" (NC-52).

Radio Moscow once said: "Therefore, from the point of view of Communist morality, only those acts are moral which contribute to the building up of a new Communist society" (NC-304f).

Saul Alinsky said "An organizer ... does not have a fixed truth - truth to him is relative and changing; everything to him is relative and changing." (www.azquotes.com)

Some specific applications of Communist morality

Lenin said: "To lie, is that wrong? Not for a good cause. To steal, is that wrong? Not for a good cause. To kill, is that wrong? Not for a good cause" (NC-355). "Promises are like piecrusts – made to be broken" (BC- 57). "Yes, of course, we are violating the treaty; we have violated it thirty or forty times" (SW7-301).

Stalin said: "Sincere diplomacy is no more possible than dry water or iron wood" (NC-304).

And **Engels** said: "Thou shalt not steal. Does this law thereby become an eternal moral law? By no means" (NC-52).

Mao said: "Morality begins at the point of a gun." (www.azquotes.com)

Although Marxists have no absolute sense of morals, to fool people they claim a moral basis for their conduct. **Saul Alinsky** said, "All effective actions require the passport of morality." So their claim for a moral basis for their conduct is deceitful. – Phyllis Schlafly Reports, February 2009

The consequences of Communist morality

This view of morality sometimes makes Communists appear self-contradictory. Examples are:

Marxists come to power in many countries by promising to take land from the rich and give it to the poor. But after they are in power, the government confiscates the land and keeps it.

Again, the Communists oppose all religion; yet where they cannot destroy religion, they attempt to control it and work through it to control the people.

The Marxist approach can be stated as: ***Find out what people want and promise to give it to them, so you can come to power over them***. The goal is to achieve power in the institutions of society so they can control the people and ultimately achieve revolution.

In short, Marxists justify any kind of lying and deceit. They may freely deny that they are Marxists, they may mislead people about their real beliefs and intents, and they may make promises they have no intention whatever to keep. All this is "moral" if it advances the cause of Marxism.

How effective have Marxists and other unbelievers been in undermining the moral convictions of our society? Are people becoming more moral or more immoral?

Obviously, not every immoral person is a Communist, but who can deny that our society is moving in the direction that Marxists want it to go? And as people become less moral, it becomes more likely that Marxists can succeed with their goals.

The Teaching of the Bible

Man is a free moral agent with the power to choose.

Joshua 24:15; Revelation 22:17; Romans 2:6-11 – The Bible teaches that man does have the power to choose what kind of life he will lead. He can choose to live for God or not to live for God. He is not just a robot whose conduct is determined by material pursuits, as Marxism claims.

(Matthew 6:19-33; 16:26,27; 1 John 2:15-17; Luke 12:15-21; 1 Timothy 6:6-10)

The Bible is an absolute standard of morality.

Psalm 119:105; Acts 17:11; Matthew 28:18-20; 7:21-27 – The Bible is our standard of guidance. The purpose of life is to serve God by obeying the teachings of the Bible. We will eventually give account for our lives to our Creator (John 12:48; 2 Corinthians 5:10).

Bible prohibitions against stealing, lying, murder, etc., are still in effect today as much as in the first century (Galatians 5:19-21; 1 Corinthians 6:9-11; Revelations 21:8; Romans 13:8-10). On the other hand, Romans chapter 1 clearly rebukes people like Marxists who, having rejected the knowledge of God (verses 18-22), end up justifying all kinds of immoral acts (verses 24-32).

Surely the fact that Marxist morality is anti-Biblical is one reason for us to oppose it.

Communist Manifesto

VI. Marxism and the Family

Quotations Regarding Marxism

The *Communist Manifesto* says: "...Communists ... openly declare that their ends can be attained only by the forcible overthrow of all existing social conditions" (page 36). Specifically, what social conditions do they seek to forcibly overthrow?

Pages 22,23 add: "Abolition of the family? Even the most radical flare up at this infamous proposal of the Communists ... The bourgeois family will vanish as a matter of course..."

Marx said: "There is no greater stupidity than for people ... to marry and so surrender themselves to the small miseries of domestic and private life." (www.azquotes.com)

Similarities between Marxism and feminism.

> **Lenin**: "...woman continues to be a domestic slave, because petty housework crushes, strangles, stultifies and degrades her, chains her to the kitchen and to the nursery, and wastes her labor on barbarously unproductive, petty, nerve-racking, stultifying and crushing drudgery. The real emancipation of women, real Communism, will begin only when ... this petty domestic economy ... is transformed on a mass scale into a large-scale socialistic economy" (LR-71).

> Another Marxist book says: "Socialism leads woman on to the path of important public activities and production work ... There are still not enough nurseries, kindergartens, and also boarding-schools, which could relieve mothers of a considerable share of the cares involved in child upbringing ... As society takes over a big share of the cares for education and maintenance of children, the position of the woman in the family will be radically lightened" (FML-603,668).

Compare this to the feminist publication *The Document: Declaration of Feminism*. The parallels are striking. Even the language is similar.

> "Women ... will be the first to understand the need for a socialist revolution ... In order to break the tyranny of class oppression it is necessary to establish a socialist order ... In the final hours of capitalism we will dance on the grave of corporate America ... Male society has sold us the idea of marriage ... The end of the institution of marriage is a

necessary condition for the liberation of women. Therefore it is important for us to encourage women to leave their husbands and not to live individually with men ... The nuclear family must be replaced with a new form of family where individuals live and work together to help to meet the needs of all people in the society" [i.e., a commune] (pages 1-13).

Alice S. Rossi in *The Feminist Papers* wrote: "The first condition for the liberation of the wife is to bring the whole female sex back into public industry, and this in turn demands the abolition of the monogamous family as the economic unit of society." – (via *The Mindzenty Report*, 5/1978 via LITE, Nov/Dec, 1979)

Black Lives Matter's official website stated their beliefs including: "We disrupt the Western-prescribed nuclear family structure ..." – https://blacklivesmatter.com/what-we-believe/ I personally saw this on the site on 6/23/2020, but it has been removed. They did not change their view, but it led them to lose followers and donations so they chose to **hide** their view ... for now.

This exemplifies the Marxist tactic of "Two steps forward, one step back." If a practice hinders their goal of domination, they may back off: a temporary strategic retreat. They do not change their view but they simply choose to **hide** their goals so they can come to power. It is deceitful, which harmonizes with their Marxist "morality."

The Marxist view of children

Marx: "The education of all children, from the moment that they can get along without a mother's care, shall be in state institutions." (www.azquotes.com)

Lenin said: "We must hate – hatred is the basis of Communism. Children must be taught to hate their parents if they are not Communists" (NC-350).

The *Communist Manifesto* lists specific measures that Communists pursue to achieve the downfall of non-Communist societies and the victory of Communism. Included in that list is: "Free education for all children in public schools" (page 25). What will they do in the schools?

Another Marxist publication says: "It is in the schools ... that the foundations for a Communist outlook are laid ... and no one should be allowed to indulge in the slightest deviation from the principles of the Communist materialist upbringing of the new generation" (NC-314).

"The basic work in Communist education and the overcoming of the survivals of religiousness must be carried out by the school teachers ... to prove to the pupils the complete contrast and complete irreconcilability between science ... and religion as a fantastic, distorted and, consequently, harmful reflection of the world ... the school must pose the question before parents who are believers as to the extreme harmfulness ... and inadmissability of imposing religious influence on children ... to maim their children morally ... by bringing them up at home on religious prejudices which are in radical contradiction with the true scientific instruction and education of the school" (NC-173).

American Communist **William Z. Foster** predicted, "God will be banished from the laboratories as well as from the schools" (NC-349).

Again, feminist leaders agree. *The Document: Declaration of Feminism* states:

"Within the structure of the nuclear family children are oppressed because they are defined as property ... We support parent controlled child care centers as a necessary step toward the feninist-socialist [sic] revolution, but our vision of the upbringing of children extends beyond them. With the destruction of the nuclear family must come a new way of looking at children. They must be seen as the responsibility of an entire society rather than individual parents" (pages 13,14). [A "village"?]

The following decree issued in Communist Russia failed, but it shows their ultimate goal:

"By virtue of the present decree no woman can any longer be considered as private property and all women become the property of the nation ... Any man who wishes to make use of a nationalized woman must hold a certificate issued by the administrative Council ... Any woman who by virtue of the present decree will be declared national property will receive from the public fund a salary equivalent to 575 French francs a month ... One month after birth, children will be placed in an institution entrusted with their care and education. They will remain there to complete their instruction and education at the expense of the national fund until they reach the age of seventeen ... All those who refuse to recognize the present decree and to cooperate with the authorities shall be declared enemies of the people ... and shall suffer the consequences" (NC-72f).

This did not work, so they backed off ... for now: another example of "Two steps forward, one step back."

Communism intends for the state to control, not just all businesses and property, but also all women and children. No one has his own wife, husband, or children. Everything is community property, including the man/woman relationship. Do you want a woman? Take your coupon to the officials and pick out the one you want for the night! This plan has never succeeded, yet it is the Communist plan.

Who can deny that Marxists, and those who likewise disrespect the family, are influencing society? Is the family institution growing stronger or weaker? Is God's teaching about the family generally respected, or is it under attack? Do people reserve the sexual union for marriage?

Are schools encouraging or undermining faith in God? Do they encourage or hinder Bible study, prayer, and religion? Do they encourage or hinder moral conduct?

Obviously, not everyone who weakens the family is a Communist, but who can deny that our society is moving in the direction that Marxists want it to go? And as family ties become weaker, it becomes more likely that Marxists can succeed with their goals.

The Teaching of the Bible

The Bible upholds marriage as a Divine institution.

Genesis 2:18-24 – Marriage was ordained by God from creation for the good of women, men, and children. It was not invented by males or capitalists. But to the extent that people disbelieve in God, we can expect them to deny the sanctity of marriage.

Hebrews 13:4 – Marriage is honorable, and the sexual union is pure only within marriage. Sexual union outside marriage constitutes adultery or fornication, and God will judge those who practice it. (Compare Romans 7:2,3; Matthew 19:3-9; 1 Corinthians 7:2-5; 6:9-11; Exodus 20:14,17)

Ephesians 5:25-29; Proverbs 31:28-31; 18:22; 19:14; Titus 2:4; 1 Peter 3:7 – Men are taught to love and cherish their wives, to honor them, and to appreciate them as a blessing from God. Such a view dignifies the woman and makes her man's honored and respected companion.

Who can believe that the Marxist view is an improvement on the Bible teaching?

Care of children is a sacred stewardship entrusted to parents.

Genesis 1:28 – God commanded the first man and woman to reproduce, but we have seen that this is limited to a husband and wife in a family relationship.

Ephesians 6:1-4; Deuteronomy 6:6-9 – Parents are responsible to train children to serve God. Children are responsible to obey and honor parents. There is not a shred of Bible evidence that the government should supervise the raising or education of children.

Perhaps the government or other people may assist parents in some specific aspects of child-raising, but the will of parents must always prevail. The government has no right to override the parents' will, to teach views contrary to what the parents want to be taught, nor to lead children to accept views that differ from the religious beliefs taught by their parents.

Surely the fact that Marxism opposes Bible views of the family is a reason for us to oppose it.

Karl Marx

VII. Marxism and Private Property

Quotations Regarding Marxism

A basic tenet of Marxism is that private ownership of property makes people greedy and leads them to oppress others. This, we are told, is the basic error of capitalism. So Communists viciously attack capitalism as the cause of every ill in society.

The Marxist solution is that the government should confiscate ("nationalize") all property and all businesses: i.e., socialism. Then (theoretically) the people own everything, so no class mistreats others.

The *Communist Manifesto* says: "In this sense, the theory of the Communists may be summed up in the single sentence: abolition of private property" (page 19). Again: "...you reproach us with intending to do away with your property. Precisely so; that is just what we intend." (page 20)

Page 24 says: "The proletariat [the working class led by the Communist party] will use its political supremacy to wrest, by degrees, all capital from the bourgeoisie; to centralize all instruments of production in the hands of the State ..." In other words, socialism.

Lenin said: "...the purpose of insurrection must [include] ... the expulsion of the landlords and the seizure of their lands" (SW3-377). And "The goal of socialism is communism." www.azquotes.com

Khrushchev said: "The powerful socialist industry, which is the basis of all national economy, is in the hands of the Soviet state and in the hands of the people. We have state ownership of land. All ... economic management remain in the hands of the state. Finally, and this is decisive, the Communist Party directs the entire socialist building" (BC-88).

Are these ideas being advocated in our current society?

Teen Vogue (7/15/2020), a magazine for teenagers, published an article urging teens to reject the concept "that any one person should own this earth's land." "While we're working to abolish the police, we must also work to dismantle what the police were put here to protect: property." "...basically we just need to abolish landlords."

www.theblaze.com/news/teen-vogue-op-ed-calls-for-ending-property-rights-decries-cruelty-of-payment-based-housing

Marxism tricks people to believe that, after the Communist revolution, the people will own all property and businesses; instead the government controls all property and businesses. But the government is controlled, not by the people, but by the Communist Party. And the Party is in turn controlled by a few elite leaders, who in turn are controlled by one man: i.e., dictatorship!

So Marxism claims that control over property and business makes people greedy, but then it gives control of all property and businesses to a tiny minority of people. What is to prevent greed from corrupting the Communist leaders?

In America, **many** people have property rights. Communists would eliminate our "greed" by seizing our property and putting it all under the monopoly control of a much smaller group of people! Communism has no solution to greed at all!

How effective have Marxists and others been in promoting socialism in our own society? Do we not see the government taking more and more control over businesses and property?

The Teaching of the Bible

It may seem that private property is an economic issue, not a Biblical issue. But look closer.

The Bible permits people to own property, own businesses, and hire workers.

Whereas Communism says private ownership is evil, the Bible expressly approves it.

Acts 12:5,12; 16:15; 21:8; Matthew 8:14; Luke 10:38; 19:5 – Many Christians and moral people own houses and property.

Matthew 20:1-15 – The kingdom of heaven is compared to a landowner who hired workers for his vineyard. (Compare Matthew 21:28.)

Matthew 25:14-30 – A man entrusted money to his servants and expected them to invest it to give him a profit. This is the essence of capitalism.

Servants are instructed to submit to their masters and serve them diligently even if their masters are unfair. (See 1 Peter 2:18; Luke 12:42-46; Ephesians 6:5-9; Titus 2:9,10; 1 Timothy 6:1,2; Colossians 3:22-24.)

But the Bible also requires supervisors to treat their workers the way they would like their master to treat them (Matthew 7:12; 20:1-16; Colossians 4:1; James 5:1,4; Ephesians 6:9).

Ephesians 4:28; 1 Timothy 6:6-10,17-19; Luke 12:15-21; Acts 20:35 – The Bible condemns all forms of greed and requires generosity in sharing our possessions with those in need.

Scripture does not require people to own property, but it certainly permits it. Greed is not a necessary result of ownership, but is a perversion of it. So God forbids the perversion (greed), but not the practice of ownership itself.

By condemning private ownership, Marxists condemn as evil that which the Bible expressly allows (note Proverbs 17:15). Yet instead of eliminating the danger of greed, they simply transfer it from Capitalists to the Communist leaders! That is deceitful!

The Bible forbids stealing.

Romans 13:8-10 – Stealing violates the law of love. But every prohibition against stealing necessarily implies the right of ownership! Why would it be wrong to take someone's property unless he had the right to own property to begin with?

So, every passage in the Bible that forbids stealing constitutes evidence that individuals have the right to possess property. See Exodus 20:15,17; 1 Corinthians 6:9-11; Ephesians 4:28; 1 Peter 4:15,16; Luke 12:39; etc.

But it furthermore follows that anyone who confiscates another person's property against his will becomes a thief. And governments can be guilty of stealing just the same as individuals can.

Romans 13:1-7 – The government has the right to collect taxes, but only for the purpose of fulfilling the rightful duties of government. Note verse 6: "For because of this you also pay taxes, for they are God's ministers attending continually to this very thing [punishment of evildoers]."

When the government confiscates private property or business, not to finance the work that God ordained government to do, but simply because rulers want to take control of property or businesses, that is a sinful abuse of government power. Rulers who do it are thieves, just the same as rulers who deliberately kill innocent citizens are murderers.

So, when Marxists justify the confiscation of private property, they violate Bible teaching about property rights and they advocate stealing! Marxists are not only guilty of lying, but they are also guilty of stealing. And we will soon see that they are guilty of murder!

The Bible nowhere advocates Communist concepts of property.

Some claim that Acts 2:44,45; 4:32-37 teach that early Christians practiced Communism. The passages describe selling possessions, putting the money into a common treasury, and distributing to others. But is this the same as Communism or Marxism? Note some differences:

(1) In Bible examples people shared because of religious motives of love for others and for God. But Communism denies religious motives, denies the existence of God, and denies the value of love!

(2) In Bible examples giving was voluntary: a personal choice. But Communism confiscates property by compulsion against the will of the owners. Note Acts 5:4. Compare 2 Corinthians 9:5,7; 8:12.

(3) In Bible examples Christians shared to meet emergency needs at limited times and circumstances. No Scripture teaches all Christians in all societies and all ages to divest themselves of all property or businesses (see Scriptures previously listed).

(4) In Bible examples Christians met the needs of other Christians. But Communism confiscates property from all citizens regardless of their religious convictions.

(5) In Bible examples donations were placed under the control of the church. But Communism places all property under the control of the government.

(6) In Bible examples people sold their property so they could donate money. Nowhere did the church own and operate businesses. But under Communism the government confiscates and operates all businesses.

(7) In Bible examples Christians owned property and businesses after Acts 2 & 4. But Communism confiscates private property to place it permanently under government control.

Nothing in these passages or anywhere else in Scripture justifies the Marxist concept of confiscation of private property.

Surely the fact that Marxism advocates stealing property is another reason to oppose it.

Lenin

VIII. Marxism and Agitation, Corruption, and Revolution

Marxists use every possible means to weaken a capitalistic society. To demoralize people they promote corruption such as drug abuse, homosexuality, sexual immorality, etc. They deliberately promote terrorism and violence and agitate conflict between classes. Finally, they foment armed revolution to bring down the government.

Some specific causes advocated by Marxists may involve an element of legitimacy. But their goal is, not to solve the problems, but to agitate the issues and cause greater discontent so they can ultimately overthrow the government and take power for themselves.

Quotations Regarding Marxism

Marxist doctrine

The *Communist Manifesto* concludes: "In short, the Communists everywhere support every revolutionary movement against the existing social and political order of things ... They openly declare that their ends can be attained only by the forcible overthrow of all existing social conditions. Let the ruling classes tremble at a Communist revolution. The proletarians have nothing to lose but their chains. They have a world to win. Working men of all countries, unite!" (p. 36).

Lenin quoted **Marx** as follows: "Revolutions are the locomotives of history" (SW3-122).

Lenin said Marxists sow "among the masses hate, revulsion, and scorn toward those who disagree with us." "The press [media] should be not only a collective propagandist and a collective agitator, but also a collective organizer of the masses." (www.azquotes.com)

Lenin said: "Only insurrection can guarantee the victory of the revolution" (SW3- 327).

Again: "The substitution of the proletarian state for the bourgeois state is impossible without a violent revolution" (SW7-21).

Again: "Riots – demonstrations – street battles ... – such are the stages in the development of a popular uprising ... The revolutionary army is needed because great historical questions can be solved only by violence." (SW3-312f). [See also SW5-147; SW10-202; SW7-18,124; Left-Wing Communism-95,140]

Engels wrote that Communists must "recognize no means of carrying out these objects other than a democratic revolution by force" (CFF-134).

Mao said: "All political power comes from the barrel of a gun." And "Communism is not love. Communism is a hammer which we use to crush the enemy." "Don't make a fuss about a world war. At most, people die... It's best if half the population is left, next best one-third." (www.azquotes.com)

Anatole Lunarcharsky, the former Russian Commissar of Education, said: "We hate Christians and Christianity. Even the best of them must be considered our worst enemies. They preach love of one's neighbor and mercy, which is contrary to our principles. Christian love is an obstacle to the development of the Revolution. Down with love of our neighbor! What we want is hate ... Only then can we conquer the universe" (NC-71).

Examples of Communist efforts to demoralize America.

Past efforts

"Harry Hay, founder of the modern 'gay rights' movement, was a member of the Communist Party USA ... Hay was also a vocal supporter of the North American Man/Boy Love Association." ("CPAC and the conservatives," Cliff Kincaid, 3/7/2013; cf. Robert Knight, "The Schwarz Report," March 2011)

The **ACLU** may be the most outspoken organization promoting the legalization of immorality in this country. They have defended pornography, homosexuality, abortion, and drug use. Roger Baldwin, one of the founders of the ACLU, was a Communist. (YCT, intro)

A man was imprisoned by Communists in the jungles of Colombia where they made cocaine for sale in the USA. A Communist told him, "The revolution is being financed by Americans who use cocaine." (CACC, 2/1/85)

Neo-Marxism: Social Justice, Critical Race Theory, Wokeness, Cultural Marxism

Classic Marxism focused on the class struggle between business owners and workers. But modern Marxists often focus on conflict over cultural issues. Cultural Marxism and Critical Race Theory had their roots at the Institute of Social Research at Frankfurt University in Germany led by Herbert Marcuse, Eric Fromm, and others.

It agitates conflict between allegedly oppressed classes versus oppressors to create conflict and alienation over any supposed injustice or cultural disadvantage: racial conflict, oppression of women, homosexuality, transgenderism, drug use, and even religious conflict.

They claim society is rigged to benefit people with privileged majority status while minorities are inherently oppressed. Disadvantaged groups are victims and should rebel against injustice and mistreatment. It combines this with the postmodern view that there is no absolute truth, but truth is whatever you believe it to be.

Evidence presented in defense of privileged classes is automatically rejected. Privileged classes are inherently wrong and must surrender wealth and power to the oppressed classes. To gain power, wealth, and privilege, the oppressed classes have a right to riot, loot, manipulate, lie, steal, or any other method.

But the ultimate goal is never to solve the so-called injustices but to aggravate and foment discontent till people become violent and ultimately support revolution to destroy a government.

Community organizer **Saul Alinsky** wrote:

"The organizer's first job is to create the issues or problems, and ... rub raw the resentments of the people of the community; fan the latent hostilities of many of the people to the point of overt expression. He must search out controversy and issues ... An organizer must stir up dissatisfaction and discontent." (www.azquotes.com)

And, "They have the guns and therefore we are for peace and for reformation through the ballot. When we have the guns then it will be through the bullet." (www.azquotes.com)

His rules for creating chaos in society include the following (does it sound familiar?):

"1) *Live by the Rule of Personal Destruction.* Treat your adversary as non-human, deserving of zero respect or compassion. ... make your attack personal, and polarize public opinion about them. ... demonize them until they are deemed Evil.

3) *Never let up with your pressure on your foe.* Always be on the offensive so your enemy can never rest and never regroup.

4) *Force them to live every second of their lives by every rule they preach* and be merciless when they fail to live up to their own standards so you can label them hypocrites.

7) *Your actions are only important insofar as they engender an overreaction or a misstep by your enemy.* Look at yourself as a provocateur whose mission is to make the other side make mistakes, again and again, until their position is untenable.

Disinformation and deception are your friends." – Sebastian Gorka's summary from Alinsky's *Rules for Radicals*, https://amgreatness.com/2020/07/29/from-alinsky-to-aoc-will-communism-finally-win-in-america/

Black Lives Matter was founded by Patrisse Cullors, Alicia Garza, and Opal Tometi. In an interview in 2015, Cullors said that BLM "do[es] have an ideological frame. Myself and Alicia in particular are trained organizers. We are trained Marxists."– justthenews.com/politics-policy/video-resurfaces-which-black-lives-matter-founder-says-groups-creators-are-trained (accessed 6/25/2020)

In a 2018 interview, Cullors affirmed her mentor was Eric Mann. Mann was a "former member of the Weather Underground charged with attempted murder of police officers in Boston back in 1969. The domestic terror group Weather Underground is responsible for multiple terrorist bombings at the U.S. Capitol, the State Department, and the Pentagon during the 1960s and '70s." – thefederalist.com/2020/07/08/black-lives-matter-in-public-schools-is-turning-kids-into-little-marxists/

"In an interview with *Cosmopolitan Magazine*, Ms. Cullors shared that she is inspired by **Assata Shakur** who was convicted of first-degree murder for the killing of a New Jersey state trooper .... Shakur was also a member of the former Black Panthers and Black Liberation Army." – illinoisfamily.org/faith/exposing-black-lives-matter/ (www.cosmopolitan.com/entertainment/a47842/the-women-behind-blacklivesmatter/)

Black Lives Matter's financial sponsor umbrella group is called Thousand Currents.

"...the vice chairwoman of the board of directors for Thousand Currents is Susan Rosenberg, a convicted felon who participated in bombing buildings in the Northeast and Washington, D.C. ... Rosenberg was part of M19, short for May 19th Communist Organization.'" – www.dailysignal.com/2020/06/25/4-things-the-liberal-media-wont-tell-you-about-black-lives-matter/? (6/26/2020)

(See also https://capitalresearch.org/article/a-terrorists-ties-to-a-leading-black-lives-matter-group/)

Marxist belief in materialism does not prevent some of them from witchcraft such as attempting to communicate with and offer sacrifices to the spirits of dead people.

"In a recorded conversation with Cullors, BLM Los Angeles founder and California State University Professor of African Studies Melina Abdulla reveals '... we've become very intimate with the spirits that we call on regularly" ... Cullors echoes ... 'I started to feel personally connected and responsible and accountable to them ... from a deeply spiritual place. ... you offer things that your loved one who passed away would want, you know, whether it's like honey or tobacco, things like that ... I believe so many of them work through us.'

"Cullors also admits that the very first thing BLM leaders do when they hear of a 'murder' is to pray to the spirits and 'pour libation' [sacrifices]. ... 'At its core, it's a spiritual movement' ... 'you kind of invoke that spirit, and then those spirits actually become present with you' ... 'Spirituality is at the center of Black Lives Matter, and I think that's not just for us, I feel like so many, um, leaders and so many organizers, um, are deeply engaged and in a pretty, um, important spiritual practice"

illinoisfamily.org/marriage/hail-satan-after-terrorizing-churches-blm-witchcraft-exposed

After a hundred rioters were arrested for looting Chicago stores in August, 2020, Black Lives Matter demanded their release. Black Lives Matter organizer Ariel Atkins defended the looting. "I don't care if someone decides to loot a Gucci or a Macy's or a Nike store, because that makes sure that person eats. That makes sure that person has clothes. That is reparations. Anything they wanted to take, they can take it because these businesses have insurance." – https://www.breitbart.com/politics/2020/08/11/chicago-blm-organizer-defends-looting-reparations/?utm_source=newsletter&utm_medium=email&utm_term=daily&utm_campaign=20200811

At the demonstration, protesters held a sign that read, "Our futures have been looted from us ... loot back" ("Black Lives Matter to Lightfoot," *Chicago Sun-Times*, Aug. 10, 2020).

How effective have Marxists and other unbelievers been in promoting corruption in our own society? Are we becoming more decent and moral or increasingly immoral?

Obviously, not everyone who promotes corruption is a Communist, but who can deny that our society is moving in the direction that Marxists want it to go? And as society becomes more corrupt, it becomes more likely that Marxists can succeed with their goals.

The teaching of the Bible

Christians should submit to the government.

Romans 13:1-5 – Civil rulers are ordained by God. Whoever resists them, resists the ordinance of God.

John 18:36 – Jesus never permitted violent revolution against the government, even when the government was guilty of severe persecution and was about to crucify Him.

But Marxists say they should overthrow the government because oppressors control it.

(Matthew 26:47-54; John 18:36; 1 Peter 2:13,14; Titus 3:1; Acts 5:29)

Christians should work for peace, not strife.

Romans 12:18 – To the extent we can influence circumstances, we should live peaceably with all people, even those who mistreat us (see verses 17-21).

Luke 6:27,28 – We should love even our enemies and do good to those who mistreat us. We should pray for them, not seek to harm them.

When rulers disobey God's word, we should tell them they are wrong. But we are never justified in participating in violent uprisings to overthrow them.

(Matthew 5:9; James 3:17,18)

Christians should never tempt or encourage others to sin.

Matthew 18:6,7 – Woe to the person who tempts other people to sin. He would be better off drowned in the sea.

Hebrews 10:24 – We should provoke others to love and good works, not to corruption and immorality. We should never promote evil or corruption, but should urge people to do good.

Surely the fact that Marxism promotes corruption and revolution is reason to oppose it.

(Romans 1:32; Ephesians 5:11; 1 Timothy 5:22; Titus 2:14; 3:8)

Mao

IX. Marxism, Persecution, and Annihilation

After Communists capture a country, they purge all elements of non-Communist thinking through re-education, concentration camps, or annihilation. This applies the evolutionary concept of survival of the fittest: people who oppose Marxist views are not fit to survive. A new race must be bred by allowing only people with acceptable views to reproduce.

Quotations Regarding Marxism

Statements by Marxist leaders

The *Communist Manifesto* says: "...the middle-class owner of property. This person must, indeed, be swept out of the way, and made impossible" (page 21).

Lenin coined the term "Dictatorship of the Proletariat" to describe Communist rule. He said it is "an organization for the systematic use of violence by one class against the other" (NC- 57). "...the revolutionary dictatorship of the proletariat is violence against the bourgeoisie" (SW-125). "... power that is unrestricted by any laws" (SW7-123).

Again: "The dictatorship of the proletariat does not fear to resort to compulsion, and to the most severe, decisive and ruthless expression of state compulsion" (SW8- 257).

Stalin said: "To choose one's victims, to prepare one's plan minutely, to slake an implacable vengeance ... There is nothing sweeter in the world." And "The death of one man is tragic, but the death of thousands is statistic." And "The only real power comes out of a long rifle." (www.azquotes.com)

Some specific examples

Statistics from Communists themselves acknowledge that, soon after taking over China, they killed 12 million Chinese. "Millions more were imprisoned, sentenced to forced labor, or sent to 'reorientation' (brain washing) centers." (CFF-63).

The U.S. Senate concluded that some 35 to 45 million people have been killed in the Soviet Union, and between 34 and 63 million people in China. ("Why Communism Kills", page 3)

In North Korea in "some areas 60-80% of Christian leaders were killed" (CFF-171).

Out of a population of 7 million in Cambodia, some 2 or 3 million died. Ieng Sary, the Communist foreign minister said: "As long as we have one million left, that will be enough to make the new man" (ibid, page 11).

Opponents of Communism are often sent to slave labor camps. (BC-62). Others are imprisoned in asylums and treated with brainwashing, mind-altering drugs, and other psychiatric treatments to break down their resistance. (CACC Newsletter, 11/15/87).

In his book *Against All Hope,* Armando Valladares tells his personal story in which he was imprisoned in Communist Cuba simply because he disagreed with Communism. For 22 years he witnessed all the horrors we have described.

So why do people in Communist countries believe in Marxism?

The answer is that most do not. Only a tiny percentage of people are Communists. Many support Communist activities at first because they believe life may be better under Communism. But after the revolution, an oppressive dictatorship controls all aspects of life.

Communists control all businesses, so if you speak against Marxism you may lose your job. The government controls all the stores, hospitals, and housing, so you and your family may go without food, clothing, medical treatment, or a home. The rulers control all communication, so you cannot contact others for help. You are essentially a prisoner. (WC-21,22)

Why don't people flee the country? Many try, but the government posts guards and erects barriers like the Berlin Wall to keep people from escaping. Thousands died trying to cross the Iron Curtain to freedom or to flee from Cuba to Florida in tiny boats.

An article in *World Magazine,* 11/2012, states that about 3000 people per year escape from North Korea. Why so few? Because many are shot and killed in the attempt. Others are captured and returned to concentration camps. Still, they continue to try and some succeed.

These are conditions after a country has fallen to Communism, so we do not see them here ... yet. But why wait till that time comes? Why not speak out now while we are free to do so?

Ask yourself this: Why is it that Communists erect walls and post guards to keep people from leaving, while America struggles to keep illegal immigrants from overrunning the country?

The Teaching of the Bible

Christians are commanded to love all men, not to harm or murder them.

Matthew 22:39 – The second greatest command is to love your neighbor as yourself.

Romans 13:8-10 – Love for neighbor means we must not harm them and surely must not murder them.

Matthew 7:12 – We should treat others as we would want them to treat us. Do you want others to persecute you or slay you simply because you do not agree with their views? Then do not do such things to them!

(1 John 3:12; Romans 12:17-21; Leviticus 19:17,18; Luke 6:27-33; Proverbs 6:16-19; Matthew 15:18-20; 1 Peter 4:15,16)

Christians attempt to change others by teaching and persuasion, not by force.

Mark 16:15,16 – Go preach the gospel to every creature. (Compare Matthew 28:18- 20.)

Ephesians 5:11 – We must refuse to participate in other people's sins, but we should tell them they are wrong.

Ephesians 6:10-18 – Christians are at war against the forces of evil, but our weapons include faith, prayer, and God's word. Nowhere included are forms of physical violence or force.

2 Corinthians 10:3-5 – Fleshly or carnal weapons are expressly forbidden in our warfare against evil. Instead, we use the spiritual weapons God has provided. (Compare John 18:36.)

2 Corinthians 5:10,11 – Ultimately God will judge all men for their lives. That is not our job. Our job is to **persuade** men by warning them about God's judgment.

If people refuse to accept God's word, we may refuse to associate with them and continue to rebuke their error (1 Corinthians 15:33; chapter 5; 2 John 9-11; etc.) But to inflict physical harm on them is no part of a Christian's conduct.

Surely the fact that Marxism murders innocent people is one reason for us to oppose it.

Stalin

X. Marxism and Earthly Paradise

Quotations Regarding Marxism

Since only a small minority in any country believe in Marxism, how do Marxists convince people to follow their agenda? They offer hope for the future.

What Communists refer to as true "Communism" does not exist and never has existed anywhere on earth. They believe the world is progressing toward Communism but has not yet arrived. Today, they are in various stages of socialism working toward Communism.

Marxists view Communism as the ultimate stage of man's existence, a virtual paradise on earth. Since private property causes evil, we will enter a world condition of universal peace, prosperity, and social justice when capitalism has been purged. There will be no stealing, no lying, no class hatred, and no need for government. (Compare FML-699.)

Lenin described this final state: "...there will vanish all need for force, for the subjection of one man to another, since people will grow accustomed to observing the elementary conditions of social existence without force and without subjection." (BC-111).

Again Lenin said: "...we know that the fundamental social cause of excesses ... is the exploitation of the masses, their want and their poverty. With the removal of this chief cause, excesses will inevitably begin to 'wither away.' ... With their withering away, the state will also wither away" (SW7-83).

Communism recruits many idealistic young people who hope to bring about this paradise. In a high school history class, I argued that the ultimate goal of Communism was good, but the problem was the means Communism uses to achieve that goal. That view was naïve, but it illustrates how Communism appeals to young people.

Imagine how appealing this promise is to young people who have been taught evolution, so they don't believe in God or in life after death. A philosophy that offers to solve all the world's problems is attractive.

The publication *Young Comrade* said: "In your religious training you are told that even if things are bad on this earth, everything will be wonderful when you die and go to Heaven ... This is all a lie. When you die, you are dead and that is all there is to it. We want our Paradise right here and now" (CFF-191).

Saul Alinsky wrote: "A Marxist begins with his prime truth that all evils are caused by the exploitation of the proletariat by the capitalists. From this he logically proceeds to the revolution to end capitalism, then into the third stage of reorganization into a new social order of the dictatorship of the proletariat, and finally the last stage – the political paradise of communism." (www.azquotes.com)

This stage of true communism has never been achieved anywhere on earth. It is the communist goal like heaven is the Christian's goal. Communists believe this earthly "paradise" is not only possible but inevitable, and it is the highest goal anyone can possibly pursue.

The Teaching of the Bible

Many objectionable features of Communism would continue in their utopia.

The Communist utopia is impossible. They say it will involve no stealing, no lying, no class hatred, and no need for government. But they advocate stealing, lying, class hatred, dictatorship, and even murder to achieve it, so why would they think all this will suddenly stop?

But even if they achieve it, they would still be **atheists** who deny the existence of God. They would still be **materialists** whose belief in **evolution** means death is the end of existence. They would still **reject the Bible** as their standard of morals. The **family would be abolished**: women and children would be community property.

For all these reasons, they would still **oppose all religion**, especially the gospel of Jesus. In fact, religious people will all have been eliminated by Communist executions and re-education. So, if Communists do achieve their ultimate paradise, you and I will not be around to see it. We would long since have been eliminated! And if our children are around, it would only be because they have forsaken their religious convictions!

So it is not just the Communist **methods** that are evil and corrupt; so is their ultimate **goal**.

The Bible teaches that most people will always be evil.

Communists believe that evolution will inevitably improve men to a state of near perfection on earth. But where is the historical evidence that people today are better than people were centuries ago? The Bible denies evolution and also denies that people will ever become perfect on earth.

Matthew 7:13,14 – Most people are on the road to destruction, only a few on the road to life. Throughout the Bible the majority of people have been in sin. (Compare 2 Timothy 3:13.)

Jesus teaches that our paradise comes in heaven after this life.

Hebrews 9:27; John 5:28,29 – It is appointed to man once to die, then the resurrection, and **after this** the judgment. (Compare 1 Corinthians 15:19-26; 1 Thessalonians 4:13-18.)

Matthew 25:46 – At that judgment, the reward of the righteous will be **eternal life**. (Compare verses 31-46; 2 Corinthians 5:10; Romans 2:6-10; 6:23.)

Matthew 5:10-12 – Those who are persecuted for righteousness will have a great reward in **heaven**. If Communists persecute us or even kill us, we will not lose our reward. The reward comes after this life, not during it.

1 Peter 1:3,4 – God has begotten us to an inheritance reserved in **heaven**. (Compare 1 Thessalonians 4:17; 5:9,10; 2 Corinthians 4:16-5:8.)

Marxists have no hope for a reward after death. Their only hope is an earthly paradise in this life. There is no evidence such a hope will ever materialize. And if it did materialize, it would be a curse and not a blessing.

The Christian looks for a greater paradise, but it comes after this life, not during it. And the Christian hope is based on evidence. We have eyewitness testimony that our Savior has risen from the dead and has ascended into heaven. He has sent messages back from heaven, and the validity of these messages is confirmed by fulfilled prophecy and miracles. These messages assure us that we too will someday be raised from the dead to dwell with our Savior in heaven.

Conclusion: Marxism, Christians, and the Future of America

What Specific Goals Do Communists Seek to Achieve to Bring Down America?

The ultimate goal of Marxists is to take over the United States. In 1962 W. Cleon Skousen, an expert on Communism, wrote a book called *The Naked Communist* in which he listed 45 specific goals the Communists sought to achieve to overthrow our nation (pages 259-262).

Consider just a few of those goals and ask yourself how successful the Communists have been in achieving them. To what extent have Communists been successful in affecting your life and the lives of your children and loved ones?

(Again, not everybody who supports these goals is a Communist. Nevertheless, to whatever extent these goals are accomplished, Communists come that much close to taking over America.)

"Get control of the schools. Use them as transmission belts for socialism and current Communist propaganda. Soften the curriculum. Get control of teachers' associations. Put the party line in textbooks."

How successful have Communists and their fellow travelers been? Do schools teach evolution, leading students to believe that they are just material animals and death is the end of existence? Have the schools eliminated God, religion, prayer, and the Bible?

Are students led to believe they can make moral decisions based on their own opinions, without appealing to God, religion, the Bible, or parents? Do schools often justify homosexuality, premarital sex, pornography, abortion, divorce, and drug abuse? Do they criticize our country as being corrupt politically and economically, so they should prefer socialism?

Do teachers' unions, such as the N.E.A., defend virtually all these practices in schools?

Remember, Skousen wrote this in 1962, long before these changes had occurred in our country. If you are not aware of the extent to which schools today are infiltrated by these ideas, I challenge you to investigate.

Seriously? Why would anyone deliberately promote ugliness? It serves to demoralize society. When people cannot see beauty and joy, they are more easily convinced to work for a different kind of life. And degraded art can be used to promote immorality and disrespect for authority.

What do we see in "modern art"? Do we see what is ugly, repulsive, and above all meaningless? Is it ever immoral and vulgar?

And what about modern music? Is it often ugly, repulsive, and meaningless? Does it promote moral anarchy, violence, and rebellion against authority?

One of the best ways to demoralize society is to promote widespread pornography and immorality in entertainment. What do we see around us? Does the entertainment industry present a favorable view of religion and moral decency, or is it polluted with immorality of all kinds in movies, magazines, TV, and the Internet?

Remember, this was written in 1962. Who then would have expected Gay Liberation, Free Love, and even homosexual marriage? But now they are pandemic, along with rampant divorce, abortion, living together without marriage, illegitimacy, and venereal disease, including AIDS.

What do we see in denominations? Do we see increasing respect for the Bible? Or do people follow other sources of religious guidance and more emphasis on entertainment, recreation, and social interests?

Is the Creator of the universe respected today in schools? Are discussions of His word encouraged? Are students encouraged to pray or even have a "moment of silence"?

Who are we being told are best qualified to understand and to treat criminals, alcoholics, addicts: churches or psychiatrists? Do courts and schools turn to religious leaders or to psychiatrists to define what is and is not acceptable conduct?

Does society look to the Bible or to psychiatrists to learn how to have a good marriage, how to discipline and train children, and even when to get a divorce? Do government and social agencies respect or oppose Biblical principles of child-raising, even calling it "child abuse."

Remember, this was written in 1962. What institution has taken more abuse in recent years than the family? Do the Women's Liberation and Children's Liberation movements respect Bible teaching about the home? Have promiscuity, living together without marriage, and divorce become rampant? What about gay "marriage"?

Are parents being told that they do not have the expertise needed to raise their children? Are they being encouraged to send their kids off to daycare, then nursery school, pre-school, etc., away from the influence of the parents to whom God gave the children?

And then if children go bad, does society blame the psychiatrists, the government agencies, or the child-rearing experts? No, almost invariably the blame is placed on the parents!

Again, not all the people who uphold these ideas are Communists. But the more these ideas prevail in society, the more the Communists benefit.

What Can Christians Do about Marxism?

1. Believe in God, trust Him fully, and encourage others, especially our children, to do the same. Diligently oppose sources that advocate unbelief.

People who truly trust in God will never become Communists. Further, if we really trust God, we will **pray** diligently about the dangers of Communism, and we will trust God to work matters out best for His people (1 Corinthians 10:13; 1 Peter 5:7; Philippians 4:6,7).

How do we get this strong faith and trust in God, and how do we instill it in our children? By the hearing and teaching of God's word again and again – Romans 10:17; John 20:29-31.

2. Understand and defend Bible teaching regarding the spiritual nature of God, of man, and the truthfulness of creation. Diligently oppose the teaching of evolution.

One of the main weapons unbelievers use to lead people to doubt or deny God and to believe we are just material beings, is the teaching of evolution in the schools and the mass media. We must combat this by spreading the evidence for creation found in the Bible and in nature.

3. Practice and defend Bible teaching as the absolute standard of morality. Oppose all sources that advocate immorality.

Communists use every means available to undermine faith in the Bible and promote moral corruption. We must be completely familiar with the evidence that the Bible is indeed the word of God. Then we must diligently teach this to our children, and to all those around us.

4. Diligently practice the teaching of Jesus, and urge others to do the same.

People who follow Jesus will avoid Marxism and every other false system. But we must follow Bible teachings strictly without any human changes.

How many Christians are truly diligent in studying God's word and praying? How many attend services regularly and actively participate in the work and of the church? How many are actively trying to convert the lost?

If unbelievers take control and deny us the right to pray, study the Bible, or worship God, wherein are we any worse off than if we have religious freedom but neglect to exercise it?

5. Thank God for the freedoms we have and pray for civil rulers.

Most of us, who have grown up in the USA, have little idea what it is like to live under the threat of persecution. But we could just as easily have been born among the more than a billion people under Communist oppression or under some other evil system such as Islam.

Let us thank God for the freedoms we have and pray that these freedoms will continue and will spread to areas where they do not exist. Let us pray that our rulers will have the wisdom to oppose error and leave us free to live godly and peaceable lives (1 Timothy 2:1,2).

6. Work to strengthen the family unit and oppose all efforts to weaken it.

Far too many have allowed outside interests to weaken family ties. Many are deeply involved in activities that may not be inherently sinful, but they are so involved that they neglect worship of God and the spiritual training of their family. They fail to resist the forces of evil. As a result, their families become easy victims of immoral entertainment, women's liberation, juvenile rebellion, and even adultery and divorce.

Christians need to renew our devotion to our marriages and likewise renew our commitment that **we** will take responsibility to train our children to be what God wants them to be.

Let us spend time together as families, pray together, study the Bible together, sing together. Let us make sure our whole family regularly attends church assemblies and classes every time the church meets. Teach the truth diligently at home. And pray every day that we will be good parents and that our children will be faithful to God.

7. Pray for the strength to be faithful and to assist other Christians when persecution comes.

Historically Christians have often been persecuted. In the Bible, God's people prayed for one another and comforted one another in times of persecution. They fled when necessary. But always they realized that they should be faithful regardless of what life brings (Ephesians 6:10-18; Acts 4 and 12). Let us do likewise.

8. Maintain strong hope for the Christian's eternal inheritance.

Whatever the future holds, remember that our reward is not here on earth. We are here only a short time. Our ultimate reward comes after this life. If Communism can be defeated in this life, that is cause for rejoicing. But if Communism or another form of evil conquers our nation, no matter what amount of suffering we must undergo, we will be victorious in eternity. Let us so run that we receive a sure reward. (John 15:18-21; 16:33; 1 Peter 1:3,4)

So, what should we do about Marxism and Communism? The answer is we should do all the same things we should do about the other forces of evil that surround us.

A Closing Illustration

A NASA photo of the Korean peninsula at night shows lights shining brightly in South Korea, while almost no lights are seen in North Korea. Such a picture does not prove whose beliefs are true or false: truth is determined by Scripture. Yet the picture visibly illustrates what our study has proved: Communism suppresses the light of truth and religious freedom, but the light of truth and freedom is freely available outside Communist countries.

John 8:32 – You shall know the truth, and the truth shall make you free. Which will we choose? Will we choose error and slavery to sin, or will we choose truth and spiritual freedom?

Bibliography

The following is a list of the books and materials which are cited in this study by means of codes.

BC = *Bible vs. Communism,* Leroy Brownlow; Brownlow Publications, Ft. Worth, TX 1961

CA = *The Christian Answer to Communism,* Dr. Fred Schwarz, (undated); Christian Anti-Communism Crusade, Long Beach, CA.

CACC = *Christian Anti-Communism Crusade Newsletter,* edited by Dr. Fred Schwarz; Long Beach, CA.

CFF = *Communism Its Faith and Fallacies,* James D. Bales; Baker Book House, Grand Rapids, MI 1962

CM = *The Communist Manifesto,* Karl Marx; American Opinion, Belmont, MA 1848

DF = *The Document: Declaration of Feminism,* Nancy Lehman and Helen Sullinger; Minneapolis Minnesota (privately published).

FML = *Fundamentals of Marxism-Leninism,* second revised edition; Foreign Languages Publishing House, Moscow1963

HRQ = *Handbook of Religious Quotations,* compiled by Samuel G. Dawson and Rod MacArthur; (no publisher listed).

LR = *Lenin Reader,* edited by Stefan T. Possony; Henry Regnery Co., Chicago.

LWC = *"Left-Wing" Communism, an Infantile Disorder,* V.I. Lenin; published in Selected Works, Vol. X, International Publishers, New York.

NC = *The Naked Communist,* W. Cleon Skousen; Ensign Publishing Co., Salt Lake City, UT 1962

REL = *Religion,* V.I. Lenin; International Publishers, New York 1933

SC = *A Study of Communism,* J. Edgar Hoover; Holt, Rinehart, & Winston, Inc., New York, NY 1962

SW (followed by volume number) = *Selected Works,* V.I. Lenin; International Publishers, New York.

WC = *What Is Communism?,* Dr. Fred Schwarz, (undated); Chantico, Long Beach, CA.

WCK = "Why Communism Kills," Dr. Fred Schwarz, (undated); Christian Anti-Communism Crusade, Long Beach, CA.

YCT = *You Can Still Trust the Communists...,* Fred Schwarz and David Noebel, Christian Anti-Communism Crusade, 2010